MY KIDS PRAYER JOURNAL

THIS BOOK BELONG TO:

Cassidy
Rose
~~Marie~~ Marie
Peterson

Jesus LOVES me this I know.

Jesus, He loves me,
He loves me, He is for me

Jesus, how can it be,
He loves me, He is for me

HI, GOD!

Date  8-17-23

Today I.... am going to praise the Lord I will be happy today

Today I am thankful for ... a nice Dad, and I'm a Family, and a church Family.

Today I'd like to pray for ... my Grandpa so he can no the Lord and I pray for my Great Grandma GG Because she is old. and Let me help my mom today

AMEN!

HI, GOD!

Date 8-8-23

Today I.... am going to Grandma to help with her Garden today. today we meditate on Gods word and serve him.

Today I am thankful for ... a home to stay in when its ~~cold~~ cold outside im ~~too~~ thankful for a church Family and a good day

Today I'd like to pray for ... Grandma Donna ~~as g~~ that she can get Saved, that we can have A good day today

 **AMEN!**

HI, GOD!

Date 8-9-23

Today I.... am going to Barb & Al's to be there and help my sister. I have a piano lesson and I am going to church.

Today I am thankful for ... food, clothes, and two pets. I am thankful for my salvation.

Today I'd like to pray for ... those who are hurting and alone. I pray for those who have lost someone. I pray for Ezra to come to church more and Matthew.

AMEN!

HI, GOD!

Date 8-17-23

Today I.... am doing school. I will help my mom in the kitchen.

Today I am thankful for ... A home and A family and

Today I'd like to pray for ... My Grandma Aunt Sara And my Grand Pa Aunt Krystal my Dad when He is at work

AMEN!

HI, GOD!

Date: 8-21-23

Today I.... ~~~~ am going to ~~~~ play with my dolls and outside

Today I am thankful for ... A home to stay in wene it is hot and cloud outside A Church Family

Today I'd like to pray for ... my Granjma and me that I can be kind to peoplo and my Grandpa that He can come to Church more every day that we have Chocg

✝ AMEN!

HI, GOD!

Date 8-23-23

Today I.... am going to be happy all day and all night and to be with my Dad

Today I am thankful for ... a home and a good good family and a mom and a Dad every day I am thankfull A home to stay in

Today I'd like to pray for ... My Grandpa and my Grat Grandma and me that I can be in Gods word more my mom and me that we can feel good

AMEN!

HI, GOD!

Date: 8-24-23

Today I.... am going to my Grandma's to help her and then we wel came home for the Day and Be with my Dad

Today I am thankful for ... A home and a family and A Church Family to Be with and A God on Loves us all Dad an night

Today I'd like to pray for ... My Grandmas and Grandpa's and my self Becouse my self I dont need this and that and peppol to go to church

AMEN!

HI, GOD!

Date 8-25-23

Today I.... going to for Be with my Dad today and play with the Dog and my mom to sped time with her today

Today I am thankful for ... A home food clothing to wear all Day and night and a family and a bad and a church family.

Today I'd like to pray for ... my Grandma that she can get saved and Grandpa and my self that i can get better and my mom to.

AMEN!

HI, GOD!

Date 3-19-24

Today I.... am going to Be a witness to my grandma i will help my mom!

Today I am thankful for ... a home and that in a couple of weeks i will Be 11 years old.

Today I'd like to pray for ... are old friend that i can help them and Be a witness.

AMEN!

HI, GOD!

Today I.... i'm going to not night with Isaiah

Today I am thankful for ... a home food to eat and that sommer is comeing up

Today I'd like to pray for ... every wone in the world to day Amen.

HI, GOD!

Date: 3-21-2024

Today I.... am not going to fight with mxBhothe

Today I am thankful for ... a family and a home and every thing

Today I'd like to pray for ... every ~~won~~ one

 AMEN!

HI, GOD!

Date 3-22-2024

Today I.... i am going to do all things in christ Jesus amen.

Today I am thankful for ... everx thing and afamilx.

Today I'd like to pray for ... everx one

AMEN!

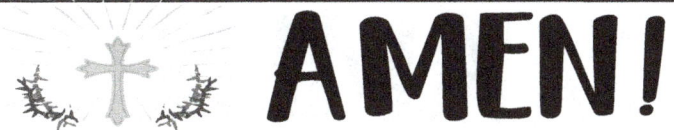

HI, GOD!

Date 3-23-24

Today I.... i am going to take a nap and to stay clom

Today I am thankful for ... my mom and Dad and my sister and Brother.

Today I'd like to pray for ... mrs. Amy and the kids that they can make it work.

 **AMEN!**

HI, GOD!

Date: 3-29-24

Today I.... _____
_____
_____
_____
_____

Today I am thankful for ... _____
_____
_____
_____
_____

Today I'd like to pray for ... _____
_____
_____
_____
_____

 **AMEN!**

HI, GOD!

Date _____

Today I.... _____
_____
_____
_____
_____
_____

Today I am thankful for ... _____
_____
_____
_____
_____
_____

Today I'd like to pray for ... _____
_____
_____
_____
_____

 AMEN!

HI, GOD!

Date _____

Today I.... _____
_____
_____
_____
_____

Today I am thankful for ... _____
_____
_____
_____
_____

Today I'd like to pray for ... _____
_____
_____
_____
_____

 **AMEN!**

HI, GOD!

Date _____

Today I.... _____
_____
_____
_____
_____

Today I am thankful for ... _____
_____
_____
_____
_____

Today I'd like to pray for ... _____
_____
_____
_____
_____

 AMEN!

HI, GOD!

Date _____

Today I.... _____
_____
_____
_____
_____

Today I am thankful for ... _____
_____
_____
_____
_____

Today I'd like to pray for ... _____
_____
_____
_____
_____

 AMEN!

HI, GOD!

Date _____

Today I.... _____
_____
_____
_____
_____
_____

Today I am thankful for ... _____
_____
_____
_____
_____
_____

Today I'd like to pray for ... _____
_____
_____
_____
_____

 AMEN!

HI, GOD!

Date _____

Today I.... _____
_____
_____
_____
_____

Today I am thankful for ... _____
_____
_____
_____
_____

Today I'd like to pray for ... _____
_____
_____
_____
_____

 AMEN!

HI, GOD!

Date _____

Today I.... _____
_____
_____
_____
_____

Today I am thankful for ... _____
_____
_____
_____
_____

Today I'd like to pray for ... _____
_____
_____
_____

 AMEN!

HI, GOD!

Date _____

Today I.... _____
_____
_____
_____
_____

Today I am thankful for ... _____
_____
_____
_____
_____

Today I'd like to pray for ... _____
_____
_____
_____
_____

 **AMEN!**

HI, GOD!

Date _____

Today I.... _____
_____
_____
_____
_____

Today I am thankful for ... _____
_____
_____
_____
_____

Today I'd like to pray for ... _____
_____
_____
_____
_____

 AMEN!

HI, GOD!

Date _____

Today I.... _____
_____
_____
_____
_____

Today I am thankful for ... _____
_____
_____
_____
_____

Today I'd like to pray for ... _____
_____
_____
_____
_____

 **AMEN!**

HI, GOD!

Date _____

Today I.... _____
_____
_____
_____
_____

Today I am thankful for ... _____
_____
_____
_____
_____

Today I'd like to pray for ... _____
_____
_____
_____
_____

AMEN!

HI, GOD!

Date _____

Today I.... _____
_____
_____
_____
_____

Today I am thankful for ... _____
_____
_____
_____
_____

Today I'd like to pray for ... _____
_____
_____
_____
_____

 AMEN!

HI, GOD!

Date _____

Today I.... _____
_____
_____
_____
_____

Today I am thankful for ... _____
_____
_____
_____
_____

Today I'd like to pray for ... _____
_____
_____
_____
_____

 AMEN!

HI, GOD!

Date _____

Today I.... _____

_____
_____
_____
_____

Today I am thankful for ... _____

_____
_____
_____
_____

Today I'd like to pray for ... _____

_____
_____
_____
_____

 **AMEN!**

HI, GOD!

Date _____

Today I.... _____
_____
_____
_____
_____

Today I am thankful for ... _____
_____
_____
_____
_____

Today I'd like to pray for ... _____
_____
_____
_____

 AMEN!

HI, GOD!

Date _____

Today I.... _____
_____
_____
_____
_____

Today I am thankful for ... _____
_____
_____
_____
_____

Today I'd like to pray for ... _____
_____
_____
_____
_____

 AMEN!

HI, GOD!

Date _____

Today I.... _____
_____
_____
_____
_____

Today I am thankful for ... _____
_____
_____
_____
_____

Today I'd like to pray for ... _____
_____
_____
_____
_____

 AMEN!

HI, GOD!

Date _____

Today I.... _____
_____
_____
_____
_____

Today I am thankful for ... _____
_____
_____
_____
_____

Today I'd like to pray for ... _____
_____
_____
_____
_____

 **AMEN!**

HI, GOD!

Date _____

Today I.... _____
_____
_____
_____
_____

Today I am thankful for ... _____
_____
_____
_____
_____

Today I'd like to pray for ... _____
_____
_____
_____
_____

 AMEN!

HI, GOD!

Date: _____

Today I.... _____
_____
_____
_____
_____

Today I am thankful for ... _____
_____
_____
_____
_____

Today I'd like to pray for ... _____
_____
_____
_____
_____

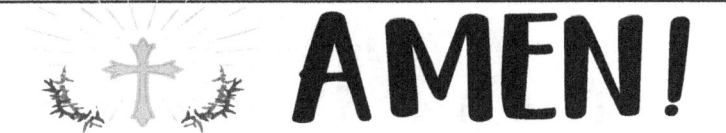

AMEN!

HI, GOD!

Date _____

Today I.... _____
_____
_____
_____
_____

Today I am thankful for ... _____
_____
_____
_____
_____

Today I'd like to pray for ... _____
_____
_____
_____
_____

✝ AMEN!

HI, GOD!

Date _____

Today I..... _____
_____
_____
_____
_____

Today I am thankful for ... _____
_____
_____
_____
_____

Today I'd like to pray for ... _____
_____
_____
_____
_____

AMEN!

HI, GOD!

Date: _____

Today I.... _____
_____
_____
_____
_____

Today I am thankful for ... _____
_____
_____
_____
_____

Today I'd like to pray for ... _____
_____
_____
_____
_____

✝ AMEN!

HI, GOD!

Date _____

Today I.... _____
_____
_____
_____
_____

Today I am thankful for ... _____
_____
_____
_____
_____

Today I'd like to pray for ... _____
_____
_____
_____
_____

✝ AMEN!

HI, GOD!

Date _____

Today I.... _____
_____
_____
_____
_____

Today I am thankful for ... _____
_____
_____
_____
_____

Today I'd like to pray for ... _____
_____
_____
_____
_____

AMEN!

HI, GOD!

Date: _____

Today I.... _____
_____
_____
_____
_____

Today I am thankful for ... _____
_____
_____
_____
_____

Today I'd like to pray for ... _____
_____
_____
_____
_____

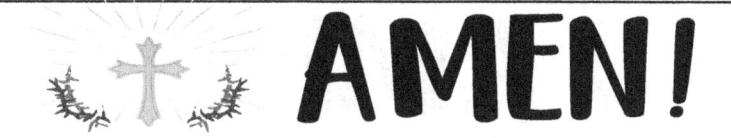

AMEN!

HI, GOD!

Date _____

Today I.... _____
_____
_____
_____
_____

Today I am thankful for ... _____
_____
_____
_____
_____

Today I'd like to pray for ... _____
_____
_____
_____
_____

AMEN!

HI, GOD!

Date _____

Today I.... _____
_____
_____
_____
_____

Today I am thankful for ... _____
_____
_____
_____
_____

Today I'd like to pray for ... _____
_____
_____
_____
_____

AMEN!

HI, GOD!

Date _____

Today I.... _____
_____
_____
_____
_____

Today I am thankful for ... _____
_____
_____
_____
_____

Today I'd like to pray for ... _____
_____
_____
_____
_____

AMEN!

HI, GOD!

Date _____

Today I.... _____
_____
_____
_____
_____

Today I am thankful for ... _____
_____
_____
_____
_____

Today I'd like to pray for ... _____
_____
_____
_____
_____

AMEN!

HI, GOD!

Date: _____

Today I.... _____
_____
_____
_____
_____
_____

Today I am thankful for ... _____
_____
_____
_____
_____
_____

Today I'd like to pray for ... _____
_____
_____
_____
_____

AMEN!

HI, GOD!

Date _____

Today I.... _____
_____
_____
_____
_____

Today I am thankful for ... _____
_____
_____
_____
_____

Today I'd like to pray for ... _____
_____
_____
_____
_____

✝ AMEN!

HI, GOD!

Date

Today I....

Today I am thankful for ...

Today I'd like to pray for ...

AMEN!

HI, GOD!

Date _____

Today I.... _____
_____
_____
_____
_____

Today I am thankful for ... _____
_____
_____
_____
_____

Today I'd like to pray for ... _____
_____
_____
_____
_____

AMEN!

HI, GOD!

Date _____

Today I.... _____
_____
_____
_____
_____
_____

Today I am thankful for ... _____
_____
_____
_____
_____

Today I'd like to pray for ... _____
_____
_____
_____
_____

AMEN!

HI, GOD!

Date _____

Today I.... _____
_____
_____
_____
_____

Today I am thankful for ... _____
_____
_____
_____
_____

Today I'd like to pray for ... _____
_____
_____
_____
_____

AMEN!

HI, GOD!

Date _____

Today I.... _____
_____
_____
_____
_____

Today I am thankful for ... _____
_____
_____
_____
_____

Today I'd like to pray for ... _____
_____
_____
_____
_____

AMEN!

HI, GOD!

Date _____

Today I.... _____
_____
_____
_____
_____

Today I am thankful for ... _____
_____
_____
_____
_____

Today I'd like to pray for ... _____
_____
_____
_____
_____

AMEN!

HI, GOD!

Date _____

Today I.... _____
_____
_____
_____
_____

Today I am thankful for ... _____
_____
_____
_____
_____

Today I'd like to pray for ... _____
_____
_____
_____
_____

AMEN!

HI, GOD!

Date _____

Today I.... _____
_____
_____
_____
_____

Today I am thankful for ... _____
_____
_____
_____
_____

Today I'd like to pray for ... _____
_____
_____
_____
_____

AMEN!

HI, GOD!

Date _____

Today I.... _____
_____
_____
_____
_____

Today I am thankful for ... _____
_____
_____
_____
_____

Today I'd like to pray for ... _____
_____
_____
_____
_____

AMEN!

HI, GOD!

Date _____

Today I.... _____
_____
_____
_____
_____

Today I am thankful for ... _____
_____
_____
_____
_____

Today I'd like to pray for ... _____
_____
_____
_____
_____

AMEN!

HI, GOD!

Date _____

Today I.... _____
_____
_____
_____
_____

Today I am thankful for ... _____
_____
_____
_____
_____

Today I'd like to pray for ... _____
_____
_____
_____
_____

AMEN!

HI, GOD!

Date _____

Today I.... _____
_____
_____
_____
_____

Today I am thankful for ... _____
_____
_____
_____
_____

Today I'd like to pray for ... _____
_____
_____
_____
_____

AMEN!

HI, GOD!

Date _____

Today I.... _____
_____
_____
_____
_____

Today I am thankful for ... _____
_____
_____
_____
_____

Today I'd like to pray for ... _____
_____
_____
_____
_____

AMEN!

HI, GOD!

Date _____

Today I.... _____
_____
_____
_____
_____

Today I am thankful for ... _____
_____
_____
_____
_____

Today I'd like to pray for ... _____
_____
_____
_____
_____

✝ AMEN!

HI, GOD!

Date _____

Today I.... _____
_____
_____
_____
_____
_____

Today I am thankful for ... _____
_____
_____
_____
_____

Today I'd like to pray for ... _____
_____
_____
_____
_____

AMEN!

HI, GOD!

Date _____

Today I.... _____
_____
_____
_____
_____

Today I am thankful for ... _____
_____
_____
_____
_____

Today I'd like to pray for ... _____
_____
_____
_____
_____

AMEN!

HI, GOD!

Date _____

Today I.... _____
_____
_____
_____
_____

Today I am thankful for ... _____
_____
_____
_____
_____

Today I'd like to pray for ... _____
_____
_____
_____
_____

AMEN!

HI, GOD!

Date _____

Today I.... _____
_____
_____
_____
_____

Today I am thankful for ... _____
_____
_____
_____
_____

Today I'd like to pray for ... _____
_____
_____
_____
_____

AMEN!

HI, GOD!

Date _____

Today I.... _____
_____
_____
_____
_____

Today I am thankful for ... _____
_____
_____
_____
_____

Today I'd like to pray for ... _____
_____
_____
_____
_____

AMEN!

HI, GOD!

Date _____

Today I.... _____
_____
_____
_____
_____

Today I am thankful for ... _____
_____
_____
_____
_____

Today I'd like to pray for ... _____
_____
_____
_____
_____

AMEN!

HI, GOD!

Date _____

Today I.... _____
_____
_____
_____
_____

Today I am thankful for ... _____
_____
_____
_____
_____

Today I'd like to pray for ... _____
_____
_____
_____
_____

AMEN!

HI, GOD!

Date _____

Today I.... _____
_____
_____
_____
_____

Today I am thankful for ... _____
_____
_____
_____
_____

Today I'd like to pray for ... _____
_____
_____
_____
_____

✝ AMEN!

HI, GOD!

Date _____

Today I.... _____
_____
_____
_____
_____

Today I am thankful for ... _____
_____
_____
_____
_____

Today I'd like to pray for ... _____
_____
_____
_____
_____

AMEN!

HI, GOD!

Date _____

Today I.... _____
_____
_____
_____
_____

Today I am thankful for ... _____
_____
_____
_____
_____

Today I'd like to pray for ... _____
_____
_____
_____
_____

AMEN!

HI, GOD!

Date _____

Today I.... _____
_____
_____
_____
_____

Today I am thankful for ... _____
_____
_____
_____
_____

Today I'd like to pray for ... _____
_____
_____
_____
_____

AMEN!

HI, GOD!

Date _____

Today I.... _____
_____
_____
_____
_____

Today I am thankful for ... _____
_____
_____
_____
_____

Today I'd like to pray for ... _____
_____
_____
_____
_____

AMEN!

HI, GOD!

Date _____

Today I.... _____
_____
_____
_____
_____
_____

Today I am thankful for ... _____
_____
_____
_____
_____

Today I'd like to pray for ... _____
_____
_____
_____
_____

AMEN!

HI, GOD!

Date _____

Today I.... _____
_____
_____
_____
_____

Today I am thankful for ... _____
_____
_____
_____
_____

Today I'd like to pray for ... _____
_____
_____
_____
_____

✝ AMEN!

HI, GOD!

Date _____

Today I.... _____
_____
_____
_____
_____

Today I am thankful for ... _____
_____
_____
_____
_____

Today I'd like to pray for ... _____
_____
_____
_____
_____

AMEN!

HI, GOD!

Date _____

Today I.... _____
_____
_____
_____
_____

Today I am thankful for ... _____
_____
_____
_____
_____

Today I'd like to pray for ... _____
_____
_____
_____
_____

AMEN!

HI, GOD!

Date _____

Today I.... _____
_____
_____
_____
_____

Today I am thankful for ... _____
_____
_____
_____
_____

Today I'd like to pray for ... _____
_____
_____
_____
_____

AMEN!

HI, GOD!

Date _____

Today I.... _____
_____
_____
_____
_____

Today I am thankful for ... _____
_____
_____
_____
_____

Today I'd like to pray for ... _____
_____
_____
_____
_____

AMEN!

HI, GOD!

Date _____

Today I.... _____
_____
_____
_____
_____

Today I am thankful for ... _____
_____
_____
_____
_____

Today I'd like to pray for ... _____
_____
_____
_____
_____

✝ AMEN!

HI, GOD!

Date _____

Today I.... _____
_____
_____
_____
_____
_____

Today I am thankful for ... _____
_____
_____
_____
_____
_____

Today I'd like to pray for ... _____
_____
_____
_____
_____

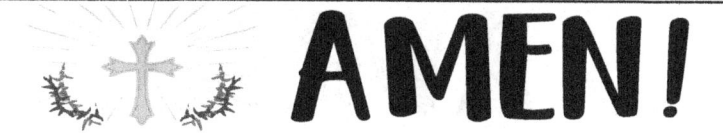

✞ AMEN!

HI, GOD!

Date _____

Today I.... _____
_____
_____
_____
_____
_____

Today I am thankful for ... _____
_____
_____
_____
_____
_____

Today I'd like to pray for ... _____
_____
_____
_____
_____
_____

AMEN!

HI, GOD!

Date _____

Today I.... _____
_____
_____
_____
_____

Today I am thankful for ... _____
_____
_____
_____
_____

Today I'd like to pray for ... _____
_____
_____
_____
_____

AMEN!

HI, GOD!

Date _____

Today I.... _____
_____
_____
_____
_____

Today I am thankful for ... _____
_____
_____
_____
_____

Today I'd like to pray for ... _____
_____
_____
_____

AMEN!

HI, GOD!

Date _____

Today I.... _____
_____
_____
_____
_____

Today I am thankful for ... _____
_____
_____
_____
_____

Today I'd like to pray for ... _____
_____
_____
_____
_____

✝ **AMEN!**

HI, GOD!

Date _____

Today I.... _____
_____
_____
_____
_____

Today I am thankful for ... _____
_____
_____
_____
_____

Today I'd like to pray for ... _____
_____
_____
_____
_____

AMEN!

HI, GOD!

Date _____

Today I.... _____
_____
_____
_____
_____
_____

Today I am thankful for ... _____
_____
_____
_____
_____
_____

Today I'd like to pray for ... _____
_____
_____
_____
_____
_____

AMEN!

HI, GOD!

Date _____

Today I.... _____
_____
_____
_____
_____

Today I am thankful for ... _____
_____
_____
_____
_____

Today I'd like to pray for ... _____
_____
_____
_____
_____

AMEN!

HI, GOD!

Date _____

Today I....
_____
_____
_____
_____
_____

Today I am thankful for ... _____
_____
_____
_____
_____

Today I'd like to pray for ... _____
_____
_____
_____
_____

AMEN!

HI, GOD!

Date _____

Today I.... _____
_____
_____
_____
_____

Today I am thankful for ... _____
_____
_____
_____
_____

Today I'd like to pray for ... _____
_____
_____
_____
_____

AMEN!

HI, GOD!

Date _____

Today I.... _____
_____
_____
_____
_____

Today I am thankful for ... _____
_____
_____
_____
_____

Today I'd like to pray for ... _____
_____
_____
_____
_____

AMEN!

HI, GOD!

Date _____

Today I.... _____
_____
_____
_____
_____

Today I am thankful for ... _____
_____
_____
_____
_____

Today I'd like to pray for ... _____
_____
_____
_____
_____

AMEN!

HI, GOD!

Date _____

Today I.... _____
_____
_____
_____
_____

Today I am thankful for ... _____
_____
_____
_____
_____

Today I'd like to pray for ... _____
_____
_____
_____
_____

AMEN!

HI, GOD!

Date _____

Today I.... _____
_____
_____
_____
_____

Today I am thankful for ... _____
_____
_____
_____
_____

Today I'd like to pray for ... _____
_____
_____
_____
_____

AMEN!

HI, GOD!

Date _____

Today I.... _____
_____
_____
_____
_____

Today I am thankful for ... _____
_____
_____
_____
_____

Today I'd like to pray for ... _____
_____
_____
_____
_____

AMEN!

HI, GOD!

Date _____

Today I.... _____
_____
_____
_____
_____

Today I am thankful for ... _____
_____
_____
_____
_____

Today I'd like to pray for ... _____
_____
_____
_____
_____

AMEN!

HI, GOD!

Date _____

Today I.... _____
_____
_____
_____
_____

Today I am thankful for ... _____
_____
_____
_____
_____

Today I'd like to pray for ... _____
_____
_____
_____
_____

AMEN!

HI, GOD!

Date _____

Today I.... _____
_____
_____
_____
_____
_____

Today I am thankful for ... _____
_____
_____
_____
_____
_____

Today I'd like to pray for ... _____
_____
_____
_____
_____
_____

AMEN!

HI, GOD!

Date _____

Today I.... _____
_____
_____
_____
_____

Today I am thankful for ... _____
_____
_____
_____
_____

Today I'd like to pray for ... _____
_____
_____
_____
_____

AMEN!

HI, GOD!

Date _____

Today I.... _____
_____
_____
_____
_____

Today I am thankful for ... _____
_____
_____
_____
_____

Today I'd like to pray for ... _____
_____
_____
_____
_____

AMEN!

HI, GOD!

Date _____

Today I.... _____
_____
_____
_____
_____

Today I am thankful for ... _____
_____
_____
_____
_____

Today I'd like to pray for ... _____
_____
_____
_____
_____

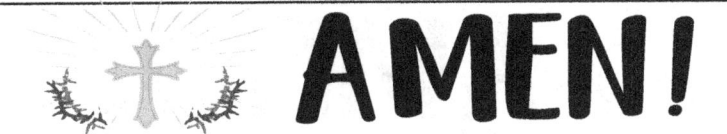

AMEN!

HI, GOD!

Date _____

Today I.... _____
_____
_____
_____
_____
_____

Today I am thankful for ... _____
_____
_____
_____
_____
_____

Today I'd like to pray for ... _____
_____
_____
_____
_____

AMEN!

HI, GOD!

Date _____

Today I.... _____
_____
_____
_____
_____
_____

Today I am thankful for ... _____
_____
_____
_____
_____
_____

Today I'd like to pray for ... _____
_____
_____
_____
_____

AMEN!

HI, GOD!

Date _____

Today I.... _____
_____
_____
_____
_____
_____

Today I am thankful for ... _____
_____
_____
_____
_____
_____

Today I'd like to pray for ... _____
_____
_____
_____
_____
_____

AMEN!

HI, GOD!

Date _____

Today I.... _____
_____
_____
_____
_____

Today I am thankful for ... _____
_____
_____
_____
_____

Today I'd like to pray for ... _____
_____
_____
_____
_____

AMEN!

HI, GOD!

Date _____

Today I.... _____
_____
_____
_____
_____

Today I am thankful for ... _____
_____
_____
_____
_____

Today I'd like to pray for ... _____
_____
_____
_____
_____

AMEN!

HI, GOD!

Date _____

Today I.... _____
_____
_____
_____
_____
_____

Today I am thankful for ... _____
_____
_____
_____
_____
_____

Today I'd like to pray for ... _____
_____
_____
_____
_____
_____

AMEN!

HI, GOD!

Date _____

Today I.... _____
_____
_____
_____
_____
_____

Today I am thankful for ... _____
_____
_____
_____
_____

Today I'd like to pray for ... _____
_____
_____
_____
_____

AMEN!

HI, GOD!

Date _____

Today I.... _____
_____
_____
_____
_____

Today I am thankful for ... _____
_____
_____
_____
_____

Today I'd like to pray for ... _____
_____
_____
_____
_____

AMEN!

HI, GOD!

Date _____

Today I.... _____

_____

_____

_____

_____

_____

Today I am thankful for ... _____

_____

_____

_____

_____

Today I'd like to pray for ... _____

_____

_____

_____

_____

AMEN!

HI, GOD!

Date _____

Today I.... _____
_____
_____
_____
_____

Today I am thankful for ... _____
_____
_____
_____
_____

Today I'd like to pray for ... _____
_____
_____
_____
_____

AMEN!

HI, GOD!

Date _____

Today I.... _____
_____
_____
_____
_____

Today I am thankful for ... _____
_____
_____
_____
_____

Today I'd like to pray for ... _____
_____
_____
_____
_____

AMEN!

HI, GOD!

Date _____

Today I.... _____
_____
_____
_____
_____

Today I am thankful for ... _____
_____
_____
_____
_____

Today I'd like to pray for ... _____
_____
_____
_____
_____

AMEN!

HI, GOD!

Date _____

Today I.... _____
_____
_____
_____
_____

Today I am thankful for ... _____
_____
_____
_____
_____

Today I'd like to pray for ... _____
_____
_____
_____

AMEN!

HI, GOD!

Date _____

Today I.... _____
_____
_____
_____
_____

Today I am thankful for ... _____
_____
_____
_____
_____

Today I'd like to pray for ... _____
_____
_____
_____
_____

AMEN!

HI, GOD!

Date _____

Today I.... _____
_____
_____
_____
_____

Today I am thankful for ... _____
_____
_____
_____
_____

Today I'd like to pray for ... _____
_____
_____
_____
_____

AMEN!

HI, GOD!

Date _____

Today I.... _____
_____
_____
_____
_____

Today I am thankful for ... _____
_____
_____
_____
_____

Today I'd like to pray for ... _____
_____
_____
_____
_____

AMEN!

HI, GOD!

Date _____

Today I.... _____
_____
_____
_____
_____

Today I am thankful for ... _____
_____
_____
_____
_____

Today I'd like to pray for ... _____
_____
_____
_____
_____

AMEN!

HI, GOD!

Date _____

Today I.... _____
_____
_____
_____
_____

Today I am thankful for ... _____
_____
_____
_____
_____

Today I'd like to pray for ... _____
_____
_____
_____
_____

AMEN!

HI, GOD!

Date _____

Today I.... _____
_____
_____
_____
_____
_____

Today I am thankful for ... _____
_____
_____
_____
_____

Today I'd like to pray for ... _____
_____
_____
_____
_____

AMEN!

HI, GOD!

Date _____

Today I.... _____
_____
_____
_____
_____

Today I am thankful for ... _____
_____
_____
_____
_____

Today I'd like to pray for ... _____
_____
_____
_____
_____

AMEN!

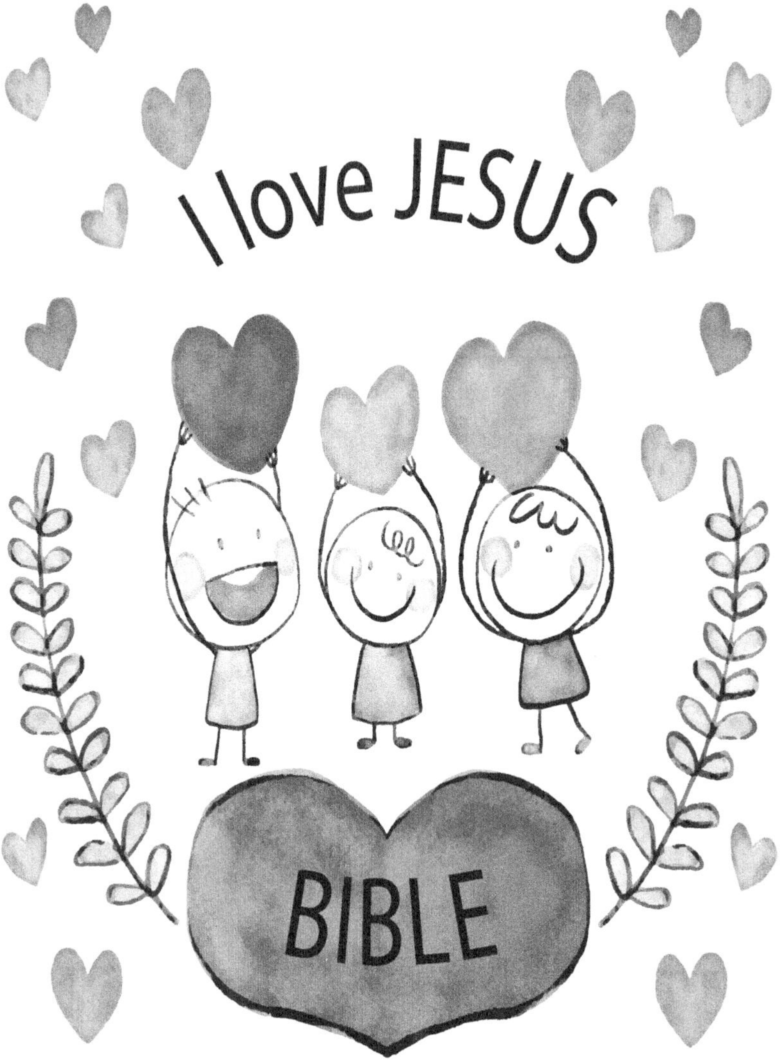
I love JESUS
BIBLE

Made in the USA
Monee, IL
09 June 2020